Yellow Umbrella Books are published by Red Brick Learning
7825 Telegraph Road, Bloomington, Minnesota 55438
http://www.redbricklearning.com

Library of Congress Cataloging-in-Publication Data
Rubin, Alan
    This farm/by Alan Rubin.
    p. cm.
    Summary: "Simple text and photos introduce some of the plants and animals raised on farms"—Provided by publisher.
    Includes index.
    ISBN-13: 978-0-7368-5986-8 (hardcover)
    ISBN-10: 0-7368-5986-1 (hardcover)
    ISBN 0-7368-1717-4 (softcover)
    1. Agriculture—Juvenile literature. 2. Farms—Juvenile literature. I. Title.
S519.R83 2006
630—dc22   2005025721

Written by Alan Rubin
Developed by Raindrop Publishing

Editorial Director: Mary Lindeen
Editor: Jennifer VanVoorst
Photo Researcher: Wanda Winch
Conversion Assistants: Jenny Marks, Laura Manthe

Photo Credits
Cover: Gary Sundermeyer/Capstone Press; Title Page: Gary Sundermeyer/
Capstone Press; Page 4: F. Schussler/PhotoDisc; Page 6: Gary Sundermeyer/Capstone
Press; Page 8: Gary Sundermeyer/Capstone Press; Page 10: David Frazier/Corbis;
Page 12: Gayla Sanders; Page 14: Todd Powell/Index Stock; Page 16: Ken
Hammond/USDA

1 2 3 4 5 6 11 10 09 08 07 06

This Farm

by Alan Rubin

Yellow
Umbrella
Books
for early readers

This farm has cows.

What do we get from cows?

This farm has chickens.

What do we get from chickens?

This farm has apple trees.

What do we get from apple trees?

What else do we get
from this farm?

Index